A ROUTINE FOR LIFE

12 Lessons Designed to Help Children Grow Spiritually and Add Value to Society. (Children ages 6-14)

MARIAN E. AMOA

WESTBOW
PRESS®
A DIVISION OF THOMAS NELSON
& ZONDERVAN

WestBow Press books may be ordered through booksellers or by contacting:

WestBow Press
A Division of Thomas Nelson & Zondervan
1663 Liberty Drive
Bloomington, IN 47403
www.westbowpress.com
844-714-3454

ISBN: 978-1-6642-3563-2 (sc)
ISBN: 978-1-6642-3562-5 (e)

Print information available on the last page.

WestBow Press rev. date: 12/10/2021

CONTENTS

INTRODUCTION AND CONTEXT

Life has many twists and turns. And in every crisis, there is an opportunity. The year 2020 can be aptly summed up as the year of crises/opportunity. The coronavirus (COVID-19) pandemic forced us to reimagine and reorganize our lives. As someone rightly said, the first couple of weeks felt like snow days for both adults and children. After a month, schools were still out, churches closed, and diners closed, yet you were expected to work and children switched to online school. I knew that I needed to create a new normal to be productive at work, keep the family together, serve my church family, and make good use of my time. I knew all that, but I was struggling to organize my life to meet the moment.

One day, in a conversation with a friend, the light bulb went off for me—routine! Create a routine for yourself—know the ins and outs of your day, however imperfect. It was going to serve as a guide for each day. I began my personal routine. Then with questions, frustrations, and concerns raised by friends and families with younger children, another light bulb went off. *Why don't I create a simple video for parents to use with their children at home?* That began my recordings on routine. The first recording introduced the word "routine" and five activities—read your Bible, pray, be helpful, be kind, and be thankful—and Daniel 6:10b (NLT), which says, "He prayed three times a day, just as he had always done, giving thanks to his God," as the memory and anchor verse. Having received positive reviews on the very first one, I created five more videos. With additional feedback and encouragement from friends and family, I developed a teacher guide, student review and practice sheets, coloring sheets, word puzzles, and other games. So it was—*A Routine for Life* came to life. This curriculum comprises twelve lessons designed to help children grow spiritually and add value to society. In crisis, an opportunity arose to meet the demands of the moment.

One unique feature about this curriculum is that both teacher (adult) and student (child) will grow as they use it. It does not spoon-feed the teachers but engages both the teacher and the student in looking at and understanding scriptures to apply them to everyday life. Everyone using this curriculum will grow. It encourages the gift of curiosity in every party.

Equally important is the fact that it is a low-to-no-cost resource. The needed materials are simply a Bible, pen or pencil, and paper. With these, anyone can use this curriculum.

Other exciting features of this curriculum include the fact that it can be used for either the virtual space or in-person gatherings. Also, it has accompanying PowerPoint slides. The student materials can all be downloaded from www.geedeecreative.com, and the videos are on YouTube at GeeDee Creative.

Finally, the curriculum is easy to use—very short preparation time for busy teachers and volunteers, and if a teacher is absent, another volunteer can easily step in to teach the class because of the additional resources.

This curriculum is my gift to our community. Created to meet a need with tried, tested, and proven disciplines. I draw from my personal experiences, and the benefits of having practiced these over four decades. It is also intended to remind adults (parents, teachers, and volunteers) about some of the disciplines we adopted in our walks with the Lord, those disciplines that helped our personal growth in the Lord. It is my hope that everyone who uses this curriculum will find it useful, insightful, and easy to use to prepare the next generation of leaders to be spiritually grounded and relevant to society.

GETTING STARTED AND USING THIS CURRICULUM

Teaching Team: This curriculum will make your class fun and engaging, and it will provide solid Bible-based knowledge. It is simple and easy to use on its own, or you can incorporate other materials based on the needs of your children. The curriculum provides you with your welcome words through to your closing prayer and amen. Another benefit of using this material is that it does not require many resources—low cost to no cost. Your children can get away with just a Bible, pen/pencil, and a notebook. Life happens, and if at any point you cannot make it to class (virtual or actual), any member of your teaching team can pick up and teach the class, using only the video if he or she chooses to.

Lessons: There are twelve lessons in this curriculum. Each lesson comprises the following:

- teacher's guide
- student review and practice sheet
- word searches/match-the-verse activities
- coloring pages
- coloring verses
- teacher PowerPoint (online resource)

If you are using the material in a virtual setting, you may want to send the students' materials to them in advance for the parents to print for their children. For in-person gatherings, you will have to print the materials for your children.

The lessons are designed to last for at least one hour. Each lesson has a suggested time for the different activities.

Additional Resources

You can access samples of the children's resources on www.geedeecreative.com.

You can watch the short video clips on the five topics—read your Bible, pray, be helpful, be kind, and be thankful—at GeeDee Creative – YouTube.

Tips for Getting Ready to Teach

- Study the lesson using the teacher guide and teacher PowerPoint.
- Test your audio materials (DVD or YouTube) to ensure they work, especially for virtual settings.
- Print the materials for your children (for in-person gatherings).
- Send electronic materials to your children in advance.

A List of Fun Questions (you can select any one or two to use for your class)

1. What are the first three things you do every morning?
2. Are you more of a morning person or a night person?
3. How did school go last week?
4. Describe how you are feeling using the weather (hot, cold, warm, chilly, etc.).
5. Describe how you are feeling using the seasons (Spring, Summer, Autumn/Fall, Winter).
6. Describe something special/interesting that happened to you last week.
7. Draw an image that describes how you are feeling.
8. How did you practice what you learned in class last week?
9. What has been your favorite road trip?
10. Would you rather take a train, plane, or boat somewhere, and why?
11. What has been your best/worst surprise, and why?
12. What do you want to be when you grow up, and why?
13. What is something in your house you want to get rid of, but you cannot?
14. Do you have a garden, or have you ever visited a farm? Did you like it? Why or why not?
15. What is the oldest version of the Bible (King James Version [KJV])

    a. What is the first book in the Bible? Genesis
    b. What is the last book in the Bible? Revelation
    c. How many books are in the Bible? 66
    d. How many books are in the New Testament? 27
    e. How many books are in the Old Testament? 39

16. What is one thing that recently made you laugh or happy?
17. What is one kind act you did for someone?
18. What one cartoon character do you admire and why?
19. What is one thing you are very thankful for?
20. Are you a morning person or a night person? (A morning person wakes up very early, and s/he is very productive at that time. A night person likes to stay late at night and is very productive at that time).

MY NOTE TO YOU

Dear Teacher,

I am glad that you have picked up this curriculum. This curriculum has been developed to assist you in bringing knowledge and training to children. It is also intended to remind you and refresh your memory about some of the disciplines you adopted in your walk with the Lord, those disciplines that helped your personal growth in the Lord.

I hope that you will find this curriculum useful, insightful, and easy to use. As you pray, prepare, and present it, ask the Lord for understanding and creativity to deliver the lessons. Take your time, be flexible, and do not rush through the lessons. As much as I say that each lesson is slated for an hour, remember that you know the children in your class/home/group and do consider their needs and learning styles.

Finally, dear teacher, I want you to be open-minded. Teaching children is beneficial to both you and to the children. The children will also teach you some important lessons. May your class be fun, interactive, and engaging. Teach them and learn from them.

God bless you as you use this curriculum to prepare the next generation of leaders.

> *For physical training is of some value, but godliness has value for all things, holding promise for both the present life and the life to come. (1 Timothy 4:8 NIV)*

LESSON ONE

Introduction to Routine
Teacher Guide

Introduction (5–10 minutes)

Welcome everyone to the class.

Check in: Ask each child two questions.

1. How are you?
2. One fun question (You can select one from the list of fun questions on page x - xi).

Pray: Based on responses, pray for the specific needs of the children, and pray for the day's session.

Memory verse: Daniel 6:10b (NLT): "He prayed three times a day, just as he had always done, giving thanks to his God."

The Main Lesson (30–40 minutes)

Goals for the day

- Children will understand the meaning of routine.
- Children will discuss the importance of having a routine.
- Children will learn about some people in the Bible who had a routine.

❖ Watch video (Optional) – Routine One: Introduction (GeeDee Creative – YouTube).

Introduction to Routine

Definition of *routine*: Routine is doing something over and over again till it becomes a part of you, till becomes a habit.

Probing Questions

Ask children these questions and have them describe each routine.

1. Who knows the word "routine"?
2. What is the meaning of "routine"?
3. Do you have a routine?
4. Do you have a daily/weekly/monthly/yearly routine?
5. Do you have a family routine?
6. Do you have a church routine?
7. Do you have a school routine?

Scriptures

For examples of people in the Bible who had routines, read Mark 1:35, Luke 5:16, Daniel 6:10, 1 Samuel 1:3a, and Psalm 55:7.

Discussion–Ask the children to describe each of these routines in the Scriptures below as they see them.

i. Jesus had a routine. "Very early in the morning, while it was still dark, Jesus got up, left the house and went off to a solitary place, where he prayed" (Mark 1:35 NIV). "But Jesus often withdrew to lonely places and prayed" (Luke 5:16 NIV).
ii. Daniel had a routine. "But when Daniel learned that the law had been signed, he went home and knelt down as usual in his upstairs room, with its windows open toward Jerusalem. *He prayed three times a day, just as he had always done, giving thanks to his God*" (Daniel 6:10 NLT; italics added).
iii. Elkanah had a yearly routine. "This man went up from his city **yearly** to worship and sacrifice to the Lord of hosts in Shiloh" (1 Samuel 1:3a NKJV; bold added).
iv. David had a routine. "Evening and morning and at noon I will pray, and cry aloud, and He shall hear my voice" (Psalm 55:17 NKJV).

Let's create a routine—introduce this list of activities as their new routine.

1. Read your Bible
2. Pray
3. Be helpful
4. Be kind
5. Be thankful

Reinforcing Activities (included resources and materials needed)

Select any or all the listed activities for the children to work on.

- Bible
- Pencils and pens
- Construction sheet/plain sheet/notebook
- Coloring verse – Daniel 6:10 (NLT)
- Routine poster
- Word search (2)– Ages 6–10, 10–15
- Student review and practice sheet

Conclusion (10–15 minutes)

Check for understanding: Ask each child what they learned and how they are going to apply it in their lives.

Life-Giver challenge: Ask each child to add to the suggested list and create their routine. Ask them to keep notes or check marks on what they do each day.

Affirmation: Let the children know how proud you are of them and appreciate their participation, their contribution, and their attention.

Altar call: Make an altar call. Ask the children if any of them want to give their lives to Christ. Make the invitation.

Pray: Model prayer, ask one child to pray. Provide prompts. Pray for all the children, commit them into God's hands, and bless their week.

Introduction to Routine
Student Review and Practice Sheet

What is Routine?

Routine is doing something over and over again till it becomes a part of you, till it becomes a habit.

Our Routine

(1) Read your Bible
(2) Pray
(3) Be kind
(4) Be helpful
(5) Be thankful

Scriptures: Mark 1:35, Luke 5:16, Daniel 6:10, 1 Sam 1:3, Psalm 55:17.

Memory verse: Daniel 6:10b (NLT): "He prayed three times a day, just as he had always done, giving thanks to his God."

Life-Giver challenge: Create your routine by adding to our routine list. Keep notes or check marks on what you do each day.

What I learned today:

_____

_____

_____

What I plan to do:

_____

_____

_____

A Routine for Life Poster

Daniel 6:10 NLT

"But when Daniel learned that the law had been signed, he went home and knelt down as usual in his upstairs room, with its windows open toward Jerusalem. He prayed three times a day, just as he had always done, giving thanks to his God." Daniel 6:10 NLT

Introduction to Routine
(ages 6 – 10)

Word List

1. Read   2. Bible   3. Pray   4. Kind   5. Help   6. Thankful   7. Habit   8. Usual
9. Often   10. Jesus   11. God   12. Three   13. Times   14. Routine   15. Voice

```
W  U  X  O  J  F  U  W  F  B  Z  U  B  A  C  J
M  T  Q  K  X  R  R  M  F  P  O  B  Q  H  I  B
U  X  C  R  A  T  Z  Q  P  H  R  S  L  Y  C  G
Y  T  S  D  K  R  A  P  A  F  E  D  K  J  U  Q
T  G  Y  S  X  Z  D  O  Y  M  K  L  I  T  U  Z
V  F  G  T  K  Y  Q  F  I  V  I  M  P  W  R  B
F  X  X  O  Q  J  J  T  H  R  E  E  F  A  V  L
M  F  E  H  V  V  R  E  A  D  H  B  K  V  R  V
X  A  T  U  Y  K  O  N  S  Z  G  L  I  D  U  O
T  H  A  N  K  F  U  L  K  U  T  O  N  B  B  I
B  V  T  G  A  W  T  S  K  O  S  Y  D  H  L  C
Z  U  T  N  F  Q  I  V  A  A  R  P  R  A  Y  E
F  T  A  L  C  Z  N  E  R  X  B  F  U  B  L  R
L  D  J  N  O  U  E  L  D  H  I  S  C  I  U  A
E  W  T  U  I  T  J  C  W  H  U  U  I  T  E  B
R  A  M  N  S  O  C  I  K  W  D  G  F  P  O  Y
```

Introduction to Routine
(ages 10–14)

Word List

1. Read 2. Bible 3. Pray 4. Kind 5. Help 6. Thankful 7. Always
8. Daniel 9. Jesus 10. Habit 11. Voice 12. Weekly 13. Family
14. Worship 15. Usual 16. Morning 17. Evening 18. Routine
19. Elkanah 20. God

```
C G A D A H U R M E I I D P R Z
W O R S H I P C W L S A X P A E
G D A N I E L D U K R Z R T K L
J H Z D H V V F D U V C Y N L K
Y I P G W E K P L E H H B W X W
X C S V L N L X X T I S V H T Y
E U Q N A I G P S V F B C S F U
E Y G H C N A X H X G W S K A D
C N T N I G F H A X K P V N M W
Z M Q N O D C R A L W A Y S I E
W A R Z B H Z Q R B I V V N L E
K O N C L U K N L F I I O B Y K
M Z B F H K S F R O U T I N E L
I L G P J I I U E E V B C O A Y
S K C E L K A N A H V J E S U S
N W N R B W F I D L L O P R A Y
```

LESSON TWO

Daniel's Routine
Teacher Guide

Introduction (10–15 minutes)

Welcome everyone to the class.

Check in: Ask every child two questions.

1. How are you?
2. One fun question (You can select one from the list of fun questions on page x - xi).

Pray: Based on responses, pray for the specific needs of the children, and pray for the day's session.

Review: Review previous lesson and challenge.

Check for understanding of routine and ask whether they followed the suggested routine—read your Bible, pray, be kind, be helpful, and be thankful.

- **Reminder:** Routine is doing something over and over again till it becomes a part of you, till it becomes a habit.

Memory verse: Daniel 6:10b (NLT): "He prayed three times a day, just as he had always done, giving thanks to his God."

Always congratulate/encourage them as needed.

The Main Lesson (30–40 minutes)

Goals for the day

- Children will have a deeper understanding of routine.
- Children will study Daniel's routine.

❖ Watch video (Optional) – Routine One: Introduction (GeeDee Creative – YouTube).

Daniel's Routine

Scripture: Read Daniel chapter 6

Discussion (guiding questions)

1. What is the story about?
2. How would you describe the lawmakers?
3. How would you describe Daniel?
4. What was Daniel's routine, and why was this routine important to him?
5. What would you have done if you were Daniel?

Reinforcing Activities (included resources and materials needed)

Select any or all the listed activities for the children to work on.

- Bible
- Pencils and pens
- Construction sheet/plain sheet/notebook
- Coloring sheet (2) – Daniel 6:10
- Word search (2) – Ages 6–10, 10–15
- Student review and practice sheet

Conclusion (10–15 minutes)

Check for understanding: Ask each child what they learned and how they are going to apply it in their lives.

Life-Giver challenge: Ask the children to re-read Daniel chapter 1. Ask them to come up with at least three things they have learned about Daniel. *Remind the children to continue tracking their routines.*

Affirmation: Let the children know how proud you are of them and appreciate their participation, their contribution, and their attention.

Altar call: Make an altar call. Ask the children if any of them want to give their lives to Christ. Make the invitation.

Pray: Model prayer. Ask one child to pray. Provide prompts. Pray for all the children, commit them into God's hands, and bless their week.

Daniel's Routine
Student Review and Practice Sheet

What is Routine? Routine is doing something over and over again till it becomes a part of you, till it becomes a habit.

Our Routine

(1) Read your Bible
(2) Pray
(3) Be kind
(4) Be helpful
(5) Be thankful

Read: Daniel chapter 6.

Memory verse: Daniel 6:10b (NLT): "He prayed three times a day, just as he had always done, giving thanks to his God."

Life-Giver challenge: Write down three things you learned about Daniel. Keep track of your routine. Keep notes or check marks on what you do each day.

What I learned today:

_____

_____

_____

What I plan to do:

_____

_____

_____

Daniel prayed three times a day (Daniel 6:10). Version 1

Daniel prayed three times a day (Daniel 6:10). Version 2

Daniel's Routine
(ages 6 – 10)

Word List

1. Law   2. Daniel   3. Three   4. Times   5. Usual   6. Room   7. Home
8. Routine   9. Lion   10. Den   11. Kind   12. Help   13. Thankful
14. Pray   15. Read

```
T Y C N U R O T Y D T Y M F P A
F I W U P O V B I W Z A C H S H
J Q P L J Q D N E N O A K Q X C
V S L U P N F E J C E D A F X R
N Q Q L I O N K L P V Q E Q P V
R H B K N I K L L U E I R N C C
A N L I T H A N K F U L J L Q N
Z Y K U A E H G U F O U E U O B
B R O S O T D N S F Z C I H J P
I R O O M E W H U D E D D E N I
C E D K H Y E N A Y T W E L J H
O A Y D A N I E L M U R Q P A U
S D M R A T Z H S U H R E Y A W
S N P B P K T Y N T I M E S H H
P Q O L C T A V Q W O K G N L S
D O D W S M M O X H B I I R D F
```

LESSON TWO

Daniel's Routine
(ages 10 − 14)

__Word List__

1. Daniel   2. Faithful   3. Decree   4. Upstairs   5. Room   6. Home   7. Routine
8. Thankful   9. Helpful   10. Kind   11. Pray   12. Bible   13. Lion   14. Usual
15. Habit   16. Three   17. Times   18. King   19. God   20. Learned

---

```
M F K K E U X E H Z Y G G Q M M
A E Q S W G E O K V C K E H I H
D U U K B W T X B W K P T B Z
G E R T I M E S H M C I H B L C
S G C H B N G F A I T H F U L B
V A I R L S D N N A A Q Q S L M
T T H E E O Z H K F C C R U E E
I S O E J E Z B F X F I W A F C
N Q M R C A N S U C A T A L I Q
F L E A R N E D L T A J E P S C
D W P E O B W N S H Z I T L D V
U K J Z U D G P M B N M T Y T N
A J E W T N U O S A M I I N Y Q
M E C S I J O N D J B O O A V O
S O Z K N R Q Q F A O I R F W B
F N G E E J I P H E L P F U L U
```

LESSON THREE

Read Your Bible Teacher Guide

Introduction (10 – 15 minutes)

Welcome everyone to the class.

Check-in: Ask every child two questions.

1. How are you?
2. One fun question (You can select one from the list of fun questions on page x - xi).

Pray: Based on responses, pray for the specific needs of the children, and pray for the day's session.

Check for understanding of routine and ask whether they followed the suggested routine – Read your Bible, Pray, Be Kind, Be Helpful, and Be Thankful.

- **Reminder**: Routine is doing something over and over again till it becomes a part of you, till it becomes a habit.

Review: Lesson Two and Life-Giver challenge on Daniel's Routine.

Memory Verse: Daniel 6:10b (NLT): "He prayed three times a day, just as he had always done, giving thanks to his God."

Always Congratulate/Encourage them as needed.

The Main Lesson (30-40 minutes)

Goals for the day

- Children will understand the importance of reading the Bible.
- Children will understand the benefits of reading the Bible.

❖ Watch video (Optional) – Routine: Read your Bible (GeeDee Creative – YouTube).

Read Your Bible

Probing Questions

Ask the children these questions.

1. Do you have a Bible?
2. Do you read your Bible?
3. How many of you read your Bible every day?
4. How often do you read your Bible?
5. Do you know there are many versions of the Bible? (KJV, RSV, NIV, NLT, NKJV, etc.)
6. What is your favorite version and why?

Scriptures – Joshua 1:8; Psalm 119:11; Ps 119:105

Joshua 1:8 (AMP): "This Book of the Law shall not depart from your mouth, but you shall read [and meditate on] it day and night, so that you may be careful to do [everything] in accordance with all that is written in it; for then you will make your way prosperous, and then you will be successful."

Psalm 119:105 (AMP): "Your word is a lamp to my feet and a light to my path."

Psalm 119:11 (AMP): "Your word I have treasured and stored in my heart, that I may not sin against you."

Discussion (guiding questions)

1. Briefly explain the book of the law and the Bible. (*The Book of the Law - A reference to Scripture, specifically Genesis through Deuteronomy written by Moses*).
2. What is the difference between 'read' and 'meditate'? "*Reading is primarily assimilation of facts without application. In other words, it is for gathering of*

information. When we meditate on the Word of God, we seek to make personal application of the Scriptures to our own lives and circumstances. This results in more than the intake of information; it transforms by leading to the formation of the individual into Christ likeness."[1]

3. Why do you think Joshua 1:8 says day and night?

4. Why is it important to read your Bible? (refer to Psalm 119:105 and Psalm 119:11)

    a. A Lamp to my feet
    b. A Light to my path
    c. That I may not sin against you
    d. I will be successful.

Reinforcing Activities (included resources and materials needed)

Select any or all the listed activities for the children to work on.

- Bible
- Pencils and pens
- Construction sheet/plain sheet/notebook
- Coloring sheet– Read your Bible
- Bible verse coloring words – Joshua 1:8
- Word search (2) – Ages 6-10, 10-14
- Student review and practice sheet

Conclusion (10 – 15 minutes)

Check for understanding: Ask each child what they learned and how they are going to apply it in their lives.

Life-Giver challenge: Introduce the children to Journaling. For the next seven days they should write the date, the verse or passage they read, and the version of the Bible they read. *Remind the children to continue tracking their routines.*

Affirmation: Let the children know how proud you are of them and appreciate their participation, their contribution, and their attention.

---

[1] https://billygraham.org/answer/what-is-the-difference-between-bible-reading-and-bible-meditation/

Altar call: Make an altar call. Ask the children if any of them wants to give their lives to Christ. Make the invitation.

Closing prayer: Model prayer, ask one child to pray. Provide prompts. Pray for all the children, commit them into God's hands, and bless their week.

Read Your Bible
Student Review and Practice Sheet

What is Routine? Routine is doing something over and over again till it becomes a part of you, till it becomes a habit.

Our Routine

(1) Read your Bible
(2) Pray
(3) Be kind
(4) Be helpful
(5) Be thankful

Read: Joshua 1:8a (AMP): "This Book of the Law shall not depart from your mouth, but you shall read (and meditate on) it day and night ..."

Memory verse: Dan 6:10b (NLT): "He prayed three times a day, just as he had always done, giving thanks to his God."

Life-Giver challenge: Start a journal entry of your Bible reading. For the next seven days, read your Bible, write the date, the verse or passage, and the version.

What I learned today:

_____

_____

_____

What I plan to do:

_____

_____

_____

Joshua 1:8 AMP

"This Book of the Law shall not depart from your mouth, but you shall read [and meditate on] it day and night, so that you may be careful to do [everything] in accordance with all that is written in it; for then you will make your way prosperous, and then you will be successful."

Joshua 1:8 AMP

LESSON THREE

Read your Bible

LESSON THREE

Read Your Bible
(ages 6–10)

Word List

1. Book   2. Word   3. Help   4. Make   5. One   6. Law   7. God   8. Night
9. Good   10. Kind   11. Read   12. Way   13. Thank   14. Day   15. Bible

---

```
D  F  R  P  L  J  N  J  H  F  C  D  V  T  W  S
Q  P  L  M  J  N  B  C  F  D  R  S  X  Z  S  T
Y  H  B  G  P  K  L  B  J  U  Z  N  J  T  I  Y
X  T  X  Y  T  I  S  D  W  H  Y  W  S  B  N  K
M  N  I  Y  O  N  E  H  V  A  B  B  N  C  W  I
J  E  X  R  L  D  I  B  W  T  I  U  E  A  Z  U
Q  U  D  O  M  I  P  G  O  O  D  O  Z  Y  I  L
E  L  M  N  W  V  F  O  H  V  R  B  A  L  I  Z
Y  Q  L  Q  K  I  E  D  P  T  H  D  N  J  E  Q
A  Y  M  O  B  U  G  T  K  H  W  M  M  Z  P  G
M  Y  O  Z  E  X  I  I  V  A  E  Y  B  R  H  K
M  B  J  A  X  U  H  W  M  N  Y  J  D  A  U  S
X  A  I  D  L  D  W  L  B  K  B  R  R  I  I  L
V  H  K  B  F  A  T  O  A  D  Z  J  B  V  O  S
S  T  H  E  L  P  U  O  P  V  E  D  Q  K  R  T
U  P  Q  G  R  E  A  D  S  S  S  O  I  L  O  G
```

Read Your Bible
(ages 10–14)

Word List

1. Apply   2. Depart   3. Thankful   4. Word   5. Pray   6. Routine   7. Book
8. Understand   9. Prosperous   10. Learn   11. Good   12. Read   13. Friend
14. Help   15. Family   16. Mouth   17. Success   18. Kind   19. Joshua   20. Law

---

```
D F R P L J N P J H F F C E D V
T W S Q P L M R J N B R N C F D
R S X Z S T Y O H Y B I G P L K
Q C N O S A I S L S T E Z E V B
K Z Z R I V F P P U S N E L K X
D M T I X K P E O L Z D X A Q J
Q C V Y W A N R B J O D L K Q P
H D D L D R M O M O U T H R C Q
O R N P J C U U G S U C C E S S
K D E P A R T S B H E L P M Y J
H T H A N K F U L U R T K R W Q
J H U N D E R S T A N D L T V D
B T G R Z V L E A R N G O Y G Z
B O O K N H F A M I L Y J M L H
T W J X S G Z L K P R A Y K B M
V W I V F V S L I I N K W F G J
```

LESSON FOUR

Read Your Bible
Understand, Apply, and Share

Teacher Guide

Introduction (10 – 15 minutes)

Welcome everyone to the class.

Check-in: Ask every child two questions.

1. How are you?
2. One fun question (You can select one from the list of fun questions on page x - xi).

Pray: Based on responses, pray for the specific needs of the children, and pray for the day's session.

Check for understanding of routine and ask whether they followed the suggested routine – Read your Bible, Pray, Be Kind, Be Helpful, and Be Thankful.

- **Reminder**: Routine is doing something over and over again till it becomes a part of you, till it becomes a habit.

Quick Review: Previous lesson and challenge on 'Read your Bible.'

Memory Verse: Daniel 6:10b (NLT): "He prayed three times a day, just as he had always done, giving thanks to his God."

Always Congratulate/Encourage them as needed.

The Main Lesson (30 - 40 minutes)

Goals for the day

- Children will understand the importance of reading the Bible.
- Children will understand the benefits of reading the Bible.

❖ Watch video (Optional) – Routine: Read your Bible (GeeDee Creative – YouTube).

Read Your Bible with Understanding

Probing Questions

Ask the children these questions.

1. Do you read your Bible?
2. Do you pray before you read your Bible?
3. Do you understand your Bible when you read it?
4. Do you write down what you learn?
5. Do you tell your friends/family about what you read?

- Introduce the Three Steps to Reading your Bible

   Step One: Ask the Lord to help you **understand** what you read.
   Step Two: Ask the Lord to show you how to **apply** it to your life.
   Step Three: Ask the Lord to show ways to **share** it with other people.

<u>**Scripture**</u> – The Parable of the Sower – Matthew 13:1-9, 18-23 (NIV)

Emphasize verses 8, 23, "Still other seed fell on **good soil**, where it produced crops; hundred, sixty or thirty times what was sown. ... 23 But the seed falling on good soil refers to someone who hears the word and understands it. This is the one who produces a crop, **yielding** a hundred, sixty or thirty times what was sown" (Matthew 13:1-9, 18-23 NIV; bold added).

Discussion (guiding questions)

o What is a parable?
o Who is a sower/farmer? Do you know one?
o Where did the seed fall? (Answer: Path, Rocky Places, Thorns, and Good Soil)
o What happened to the different places that the seed fell?

- o Why is it important for the seed to fall on good soil?
- o What is the meaning of bearing fruit? (probe)

- **Vs 23: Everyone should read verse 23**. "But the seed falling on good soil refers to someone who hears the word and understands it. This is the one who produces a crop, yielding a hundred, sixty or thirty times what was sown."
- **Understanding**: It is important to ask the Lord for understanding whenever you read your Bible.
- **Yielding**: Whenever you share the Word, or what you read from the Bible, you are spreading the word. It will bear fruit.

Reinforcing Activities (included resources and materials needed)

Select any or all the listed activities for the children to work on.

- Bible
- Pencils and pens
- Construction sheet/plain sheet/notebook
- Three Steps to Reading your Bible image
- Coloring sheet – The Parable of the Sower
- Word search (2) – Ages 6-10, 10-14
- Student review and practice sheet

Conclusion (10 – 15 minutes)

Check for understanding: Ask each child what they learned and how they are going to apply it in their lives.

Life-Giver challenge: Ask the children to continue Journaling. They should include –1) What I read, 2) What I learned, 3) What I will do next (how I will apply it and/or how I will share it with others?) *Remind the children to continue tracking their routines.*

Affirmation: Let the children know how proud you are of them and appreciate their participation, their contribution, and their attention.

Altar call: Make an altar call. Ask the children if any of them want to give their lives to Christ. Make the invitation.

Closing prayer: Model prayer. Ask one child to pray. Provide prompts. Pray for all the children, commit them into God's hands, and bless their week.

LESSON FOUR

Read Your Bible –
Understand, Apply, and Share
Student Review and Practice Sheet

What is Routine? Routine is doing something over and over again till it becomes a part of you, till it becomes a habit.

Our Routine

    (1) Read your Bible
    (2) Pray
    (3) Be kind
    (4) Be helpful
    (5) Be thankful

Read: Matthew 13:1-9, 18-23 - The Parable of the Sower.

Memory verse: Dan 6:10b (NLT): "He prayed three times a day, just as he had always done, giving thanks to his God."

Life-Giver challenge: Continue journaling, include 1) What you read, 2) What you learned, and 3) What you will do next (how you will apply it in your own life and/or how you will share it with others)

What I learned today:

_____

_____

_____

What I plan to do:

_____

_____

_____

The Parable of the Sower

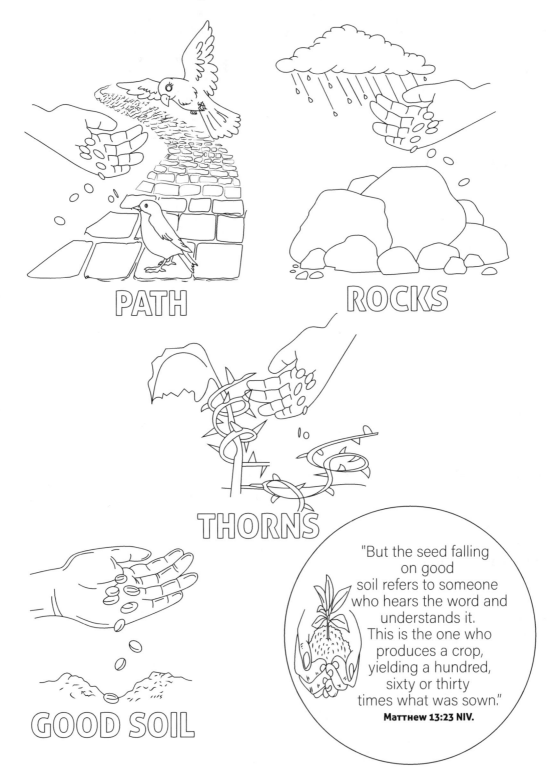

PATH

ROCKS

THORNS

GOOD SOIL

"But the seed falling on good soil refers to someone who hears the word and understands it. This is the one who produces a crop, yielding a hundred, sixty or thirty times what was sown."
Matthew 13:23 NIV.

Read your Bible: Three Steps – Understand, Apply, Share

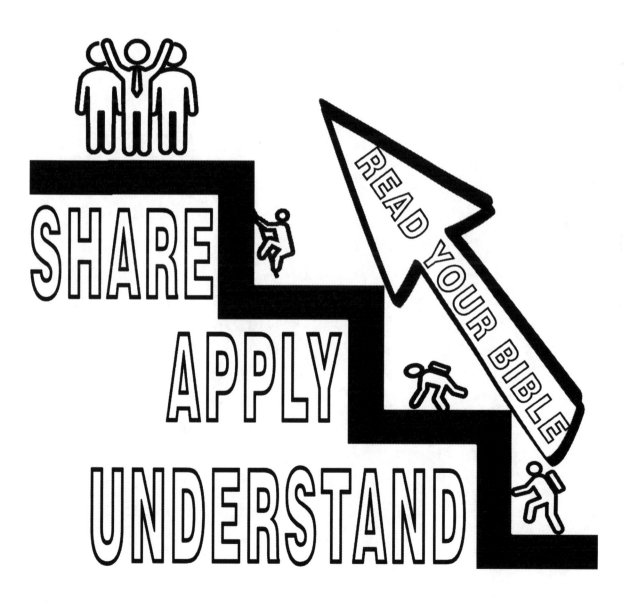

Read Your Bible:
Understand, Apply, and Share
(ages 6–10)

Word List

1. Read   2. Bible   3. Habit   4. Help   5. Apply   6. Share   7. Sow   8. Birds
9. Rocks   10. Path   11. Soil   12. Seed   13. Root   14. Life   15. Thorns

```
L P O R M W J H H R Z Z G P N H
J A O Y D Z G D C P S R P H E P
K T P R J G C N L D G D D N F W
R H J P T Y Z E H G W Z R S U J
H L Y V L H H C E C R H H S P A
N Z D D K Y A L U Q E U K K M T
Y T Q Z X T B L A R R C L S F R
H I V L C I I E A K O B E X L I
D S O W B L T H O R N S C A Z V
S A B Q C I S F Y E O W H Y P V
T M W C Z F R F S A F O C S U W
E Q U B S E E D W D D O T K S K
Z G H F O I X G S O W O U F H Q
O Q W M I X X I U S Z G E L L K
X Z D J L E D J M P V T W V Z O
X O P O C D E K G R C Y R Z A C
```

Read Your Bible: Understand, Apply, and Share (ages 10–14)

Word List

1. Read   2. Bible   3. Habit   4. Share   5. Apply   6. Understanding   7. Parable
8. Farmer   9. Soil   10. Seed   11. Path   12. Birds   13. Rocky   14. Shallow
15. Root   16. Thorns   17. Produce   18. Yield   19. Ground   20. Good

---

```
Z  R  N  C  J  W  O  H  J  I  F  M  P  V  U  W
P  T  V  A  F  G  Y  T  B  C  L  S  R  J  R  D
K  Z  B  R  D  P  K  S  L  H  N  J  E  E  G  I
T  S  Q  B  X  A  D  Q  P  Q  R  G  M  R  R  K
T  T  H  U  P  R  O  D  U  C  E  R  A  G  K  W
Q  B  Z  A  I  A  P  P  L  Y  A  F  V  N  O  D
Q  I  S  B  L  B  T  M  D  F  D  M  H  R  A  Y
Z  B  H  O  Q  L  Z  H  L  B  O  B  T  B  K  S
S  L  A  W  I  E  O  S  H  Q  Y  K  H  C  P  K
B  E  R  D  M  L  D  W  O  H  D  Y  O  C  N  U
A  D  E  N  G  L  U  K  Z  J  T  R  R  D  U  H
P  U  N  D  E  R  S  T  A  N  D  I  N  G  F  A
W  V  O  I  H  I  O  C  F  Y  E  G  S  W  G  B
S  K  Y  E  F  M  S  U  N  B  I  O  T  B  O  I
Y  F  B  I  H  H  E  H  N  V  V  W  R  O  O  T
G  R  Z  Z  U  V  W  O  Q  D  T  G  U  J  D  F
```

LESSON FIVE

Pray: The ACTS Method
Teacher Guide

Introduction (10 Minutes)

Welcome everyone to the class.

Check-in: Ask every child two questions.

1. How are you?
2. One fun question (You can select one from the list of fun questions on page x - xi).

Pray: Based on responses, pray for the specific needs of the children, and pray for the day's session.

Quick Review: Previous lesson and challenge on 'Read your Bible: Understand, Apply, and Share.'

Check for understanding of routine and ask whether they followed the suggested routine – Read your Bible, Pray, Be Kind, Be Helpful, and Be Thankful.

• **Reminder:** Routine is doing something over and over again till it becomes a part of you, till becomes a habit.

Memory Verse: Daniel 6:10b (NLT): "He prayed three times a day, just as he had always done, giving thanks to his God."

Always Congratulate/Encourage them as needed.

The Main Lesson (30 - 40minutes)

Goals for the day

- Children will understand what it means to pray/what prayer is.
- Children will understand the importance of praying.
- Children will learn how to pray using the ACTS method.

❖ Watch video (Optional) – Routine: Pray (GeeDee Creative – YouTube).

Pray

Probing Questions

1. What is prayer?
2. Do you know any people in the bible who prayed? (link this back to Daniel 6:10)
3. How often should we pray?
4. How should we pray?
5. Who should we pray for?

- Introduce the children to the **ACTS Method of Prayer.** This method has been used by believers for many years. This acronym reminds us of the important elements we should include when we pray. *This method helps us worship God, ask Him for forgiveness, thank God for all that He has done, and pray for other people.* This method is like a plan to help us when we pray so our minds and thoughts are not all over the place.

  - **A –** *Adoration*
  - **C –** *Confession*
  - **T–** *Thanksgiving*
  - **S –** *Supplication*

Adoration. Let God know that you love Him, you adore Him, you respect and honor Him (Matthew 6:9)
Confession. Ask God for forgiveness – for disobedience, your bad or wrong attitude, sins, etc. (1 John 1:8- 9, Matthew 6:12)
Thanksgiving. Thank God for all that He has done for you and for other people (Psalm 9:1, Luke 17:15-16)
Supplication. Pray for all the things you need, the needs of your friends, family, and others (Matthew 6:11, 1 Timothy 2:1-2, Philippians 4:6-7)

Scriptures: Philippians 4:6 (*NB: Read all the verses for each of the letters in the ACTS method if you have time.*)

Reinforcing Activities (included resources and materials needed)

Select any or all the listed activities for the children to work on.

- Bible
- Pencils and Pens
- Construction sheet/plain sheet/notebook
- Pray – The ACTS Method image
- Coloring verse– Philippians 4:6
- Word search (2) – Ages 6-10, 10-14
- Student review and practice sheet

Conclusion (10 - 15 minutes)

Check for understanding: Ask each child what they learned and how they are going to apply it in their lives.

Life-Giver challenge: Pray using the ACTS method. Write in your journal each time you use it to pray. *Remind the children to continue tracking their routine.*

Affirmation: Let the children know how proud you are of them and appreciate their participation, their contribution, and their attention.

Altar call: Make an altar call. Ask the children if any of them want to give their lives to Christ. Make the invitation.

Closing prayer: Model prayer. Ask one child to pray. Provide prompts. Pray for all the children, commit them into God's hands, and bless their week.

Pray: The ACTS Method
Student Review and Practice Sheet

What is Routine? Routine is doing something over and over again till it becomes a part of you, till becomes a habit.

Our Routine

(1) Read your Bible
(2) Pray
(3) Be kind
(4) Be helpful
(5) Be thankful

Read: 1 Thessalonians 5:17, Philippians 4:6.

Memory verse: Dan 6:10b (NLT): "He prayed three times a day, just as he had always done, giving thanks to his God."

Life-Giver challenge: Pray using the ACTS method. Write in your journal, each time you use this method to pray.

What I learned today:

_____

_____

_____

What I plan to do:

_____

_____

_____

LESSON FIVE

Philippians 4:6 NLT

Don't worry about anything;

Pray About

Everything.

Tell God what you need,

and thank him for all he

has done.

Philippians 4:6 NLT

The ACTS Method of Prayer

1 **A**doration.
Let God know that you love Him, you adore Him, you respect and honor Him.
Matthew 6:9

2 **C**onfession.
Ask God for forgiveness – for disobedience, your bad or wrong attitude, sins, etc.
1 John 1:8- 9, Matthew 6:12

3 **T**hanksgiving.
Thank God for all that He has done for you and for other people.
Psalm 9:1, Luke 17:15-16

4 **S**upplication.
Pray for all the things you need, the needs of your friends, family, and others.
Matthew 6:11, 1 Timothy 2:1-2, Philippians 4:6-7

Pray: The ACTS Method
(ages 6–10)

Word List

1. Pray   2. Three   3. Times   4. Always   5. Done   6. Habit   7. Thanks
8. Adore   9. Confess   10. Need   11. Friends   12. Family   13. Sins
14. God   15. Ask

```
A  X  B  G  X  U  Z  N  A  W  A  B  E  T  E  Z
S  Q  W  E  Y  Q  C  I  V  G  T  H  N  O  X  U
M  K  K  J  I  E  K  C  P  I  R  T  M  J  S  D
L  K  E  U  Q  P  G  N  K  V  S  L  R  N  B  R
C  Z  M  Z  G  T  O  T  I  F  A  M  I  L  Y  V
Q  O  O  G  U  H  P  P  Z  J  R  S  W  L  C  H
W  I  N  T  H  A  E  G  W  A  P  I  O  P  S  S
B  X  J  F  E  N  T  G  T  H  R  E  E  U  J  D
P  N  G  J  E  K  K  V  I  A  A  Q  Y  N  L  L
W  Z  O  U  U  S  Q  S  M  B  Y  S  B  E  D  I
X  I  H  B  A  V  S  N  E  I  T  S  G  E  O  S
U  P  P  R  L  D  S  D  S  T  E  H  U  D  N  N
X  J  P  Y  W  P  O  C  T  S  D  H  C  S  E  M
B  E  M  M  A  G  V  R  I  M  K  W  C  Y  S  Q
W  G  I  W  Y  P  N  V  E  F  U  S  S  Y  S  F
I  C  J  M  S  P  N  I  O  L  F  G  I  Z  I  C
```

Pray: The ACTS Method
(ages 10–14)

Word List

1. Pray 2. Three 3. Times 4. Always 5. Adoration 6. Confession
7. Thanksgiving 8. Supplication 9. Needs 10. Friends 11. Family
12. Forgiveness 13. Routine 14. Sins 15. God 16. Father 17. Habit
18. Ask 19. Everything 20. Request

```
G E T C C C X J A D K G S W P B
A D O R A T I O N H I C U P L Y
A A J E W H I Q W S G O D Q A O
Q H N V B A T I S U S N T H L D
R O U T I N E N Y P N F H T R A
H T E D E K I A A P E R I E T
R E Q U E S T T X L R S E F O S
D V M J R G T C O I A S E D B G
F E P M X I D Y F C Y I M X S C
Q R M V B V L B W A R O T M W N
Q Y Z A J I C I W T T N I V C D
O T H H M N Q L O I B H M P L F
N H Y A O G A S K O R D E W V H
Q I F O R G I V E N E S S R C L
K N N W M Z N E L P R D X T K U
P G F F R I E N D S G N P X J V
```

Pray: The Five Finger Prayer Guide Teacher Guide

Introduction (10 Minutes)

Welcome everyone to the class.

Check-in: Ask every child two questions.

1. How are you?
2. One fun question (You can select one from the list of fun questions on page x - xi).

Pray: Based on responses, pray for the specific needs of the children, and pray for the day's session.

Check for understanding of routine and ask whether they followed the suggested routine – Read your Bible, Pray, Be Kind, Be Helpful, and Be Thankful.

- **Reminder:** Routine is doing something over and over again till it becomes a part of you, till it becomes a habit.

Quick Review: Previous lesson and challenge on 'Pray: The ACTS Method' and ask them what they learned.

Memory Verse: Daniel 6:10b (NLT): "He prayed three times a day, just as he had always done, giving thanks to his God."

Always Congratulate/Encourage them as needed.

The Main Lesson (30-40 minutes)

Goals for the day

- Children will review what it means to pray/what prayer is.
- Children will learn how to pray using the Five Finger Prayer Guide.

❖ Watch video (Optional) – Routine: Pray (GeeDee Creative – YouTube).

Pray

Probing Questions

o What is prayer? (review the last lesson)
o How should we pray?
o Who should we pray for?

Scriptures: 1 Thessalonians 5:17 (Ask the children about how they can pray continually?)

Tip – You can use also read the scriptures for each of the fingers.

- ***Introduce the Five Finger Prayer Guide*** – The Five Finger Prayer Guide helps us know who to pray for. It uses fingers to guide and remind people to pray.

  Thumb: People who are close to you. These are your close friends and family.

  Pointer: People who point the way. These are the leaders in your life, such as teachers, pastors, mentors, and coaches.

  Tall Finger: People in authority. These are the people in the government, the military, and the police.

  Ring Finger (your weakest finger): People who are weak. These are the people who are sick, live in poverty, or are treated badly.

  Pinky: You, this finger is for your personal needs.

- Practice using the Five Finger Guide to pray in class.

Reinforcing Activities (included resources and materials needed)

Select any or all the listed activities for the children to work on.

- Bible
- Pencils and pens
- Construction sheet/plain sheet/notebook
- The Five-Finger Prayer Guide image
- Coloring sheet (2) – The Five-Finger Prayer Guide
- Coloring verse – 1Thessalonians 5:17
- Word search (2) – Ages 6–10, 10–14
- Student review and practice sheet

Conclusion (10 - 15 minutes)

Check for understanding: Ask each child what they learned and how they are going to apply it in their lives.

Life-Giver challenge: Using the five-finger prayer approach, make a list of people you will be praying for this week. *Remind the children to continue tracking their routine.*

Affirmation: Let the children know how proud you are of them and appreciate their participation, their contribution, and their attention.

Altar call: Make an altar call. Ask the children if any of them want to give their lives to Christ. Make the invitation.

Closing prayer: Model prayer. Ask one child to pray. Provide prompts. Pray for all the children, commit them into God's hands, and bless their week.

Pray: The Five Finger Prayer Guide Student Review and Practice Sheet

What is Routine? Routine is doing something over and over again till it becomes a part of you, till it becomes a habit.

Our Routine

(1) Read your Bible
(2) Pray
(3) Be kind
(4) Be helpful
(5) Be thankful

Read: 1 Thessalonians 5:17

Memory verse: Dan 6:10b (NLT): "He prayed three times a day, just as he had always done, giving thanks to his God."

Life-Giver challenge: Using the Five Finger Prayer Guide make a list of people you will be praying for this week.

What I learned today:

_____

_____

_____

What I plan to do:

_____

_____

_____

1Thessalonians 5:17 NIV

"Pray Continually,"

1 Thessalonians 5:17 NIV

The Five Finger Prayer Guide

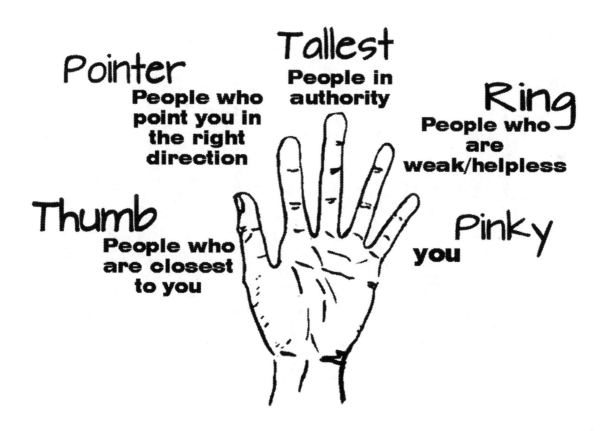

Pointer
People who point you in the right direction

Tallest
People in authority

Ring
People who are weak/helpless

Thumb
People who are closest to you

Pinky
you

The Five Finger Prayer Guide with examples. Version 1

The Five Finger Prayer Guide with examples. Version 2

Pray: The Five Finger Prayer Guide (ages 6–10)

Word List

1. Sick   2. Your   3. Learn   4. Close   5. Daniel   6. Tall   7. Read   8. Weak
9. Help   10. Pray   11. Five   12. Kind   13. Bible   14. Habit   15. Family

---

```
X  M  Y  T  B  H  S  P  F  C  G  S  J  Y  P  L
S  W  C  U  G  T  W  B  D  N  P  E  D  B  A  T
M  Z  Y  E  V  C  Y  X  Z  X  P  N  P  H  R  H
N  C  H  F  I  B  N  E  Q  X  P  O  R  O  M  E
C  N  F  B  J  A  L  P  Q  X  F  W  E  A  K  U
J  D  I  K  I  N  D  M  F  W  V  V  I  R  A  T
V  K  T  K  R  B  M  D  A  N  I  E  L  U  O  Y
N  K  R  A  G  L  L  K  M  F  S  I  C  K  L  L
B  B  E  H  L  H  P  E  I  O  C  M  R  H  D  G
D  L  A  B  H  L  L  S  L  S  I  W  L  L  H  C
V  X  D  F  E  P  X  C  Y  Q  D  N  Y  J  Y  R
X  K  V  H  O  B  R  O  N  B  O  G  D  I  T  G
M  U  S  X  A  U  O  A  Z  A  E  Y  G  K  B  F
V  O  T  E  O  B  X  E  Y  J  K  B  W  E  H  I
X  J  S  Y  V  R  I  P  M  Q  E  I  V  B  U  Z
R  T  L  P  E  Z  J  T  S  N  U  B  G  D  J  W
```

Pray: The Five Finger Prayer Guide (ages 10–14)

Word List

1. Understand   2. Teachers   3. Family   4. Continually   5. Finger   6. Three
7. Close   8. Kind   9. Leaders   10. People   11. Give   12. Read   13. Share
14. Bible   15. First   16. Weak   17. Routine   18. Pray   19. Thankful   20. Helpful

```
V  O  E  H  M  A  V  V  K  H  W  T  S  M  O  T
L  T  J  S  Y  P  U  T  I  V  B  R  H  Z  Q  U
N  O  S  X  B  G  F  I  N  G  E  R  X  R  R  N
B  U  K  H  L  C  B  R  D  H  B  I  B  L  E  D
R  V  P  R  A  Y  O  W  C  O  P  E  O  P  L  E
H  D  R  D  B  R  F  A  M  I  L  Y  K  R  S  R
S  B  T  G  I  V  E  A  B  A  M  E  R  O  L  S
Y  L  Y  T  B  T  H  A  N  K  F  U  L  U  Y  T
V  M  Y  A  H  G  Q  G  Y  Z  F  C  F  T  Y  A
M  S  M  W  L  V  R  N  W  Y  A  P  I  I  T  N
K  Z  X  K  T  F  X  U  W  V  L  Q  R  N  L  D
Q  T  C  T  D  L  E  A  D  E  R  S  S  E  C  V
U  B  V  C  Z  M  E  B  H  A  A  E  T  C  B  O
C  X  L  E  Q  I  I  F  N  T  B  K  A  K  D  W
C  O  N  T  I  N  U  A  L  L  Y  G  W  D  D  I
B  O  K  A  D  Z  Y  I  A  L  G  R  E  V  S  G
```

LESSON SEVEN

Review: Lessons One to Six
Teacher Guide

Introduction (5–10 minutes)

Welcome everyone to the class.

- Check-in: Ask every child two questions.

    1. How are you?
    2. One fun question (You can select one from the list of fun questions on page x - xi).

- Pray: Based on responses, pray for the specific needs of the children, and pray for the day's session.

Check for understanding of routine and ask whether they followed the suggested routine – Read your Bible, Pray, Be Kind, Be Helpful, and Be Thankful.

- **Reminder:** Routine is doing something over and over again till it becomes a part of you, till becomes a habit.

Memory verse: Daniel 6:10b (NLT): "He prayed three times a day, just as he had always done, giving thanks to his God."

The Main Lesson (30-40 minutes)

Goals for the day

- Children will share understanding on routine.
- Children will review lessons on:

o   Introduction to Routine.

o   Read your Bible.

o   Pray.

Review Lessons One through Six

❖ Watch video (Optional) – Routine: Pray (GeeDee Creative – YouTube). (*This video is useful for a review of the first six lessons*)

A. Introduction to Routine - "But when Daniel learned that the law had been signed, he went home and knelt down as usual in his upstairs room, with its windows open toward Jerusalem. **He prayed three times a day, just as he had always done, giving thanks to his God**" (Daniel 6:10 NLT; bold added)

- What does routine mean to you?
- Have you followed your routine?
- What is your routine – daily, weekly, yearly?

B. Read Your Bible "**This Book of the Law shall not depart from your mouth, but you shall read [and meditate on] it day and night,** so that you may be careful to do [everything] in accordance with all that is written in it; for then you will make your way prosperous, and then you will be successful" (Joshua1:8 AMP; bold added)

- Do you read your bible? How often do you read your Bible? What are the three things to ask God when you read your Bible?

C. Pray "**Pray continually**" (1 Thessalonians 5:17 NIV; bold added), " ...don't worry about anything, instead, **pray about everything**. Tell God what you need and thank him for all he has done" (Philippians 4:6-7 NLT; bold added).

- Do you pray? How often do you pray? How often should we pray? What is the ACTS method? What is the Five Finger Prayer guide?

Reinforcing Activities (included resources and materials needed)

Select any or all the listed activities for the children to work on.

- Bible
- Pencils and pens

- Construction sheet/plain sheet/notebook
- Student review and practice sheet

Conclusion (10 minutes)

Check for understanding: Ask each child what they learned.

Life-Giver challenge: Ask each child to complete take home sheet with what they have learned. *Remind the children to continue tracking their routine.*

Affirmation: Let the children know how proud you are of them and appreciate their participation, their contribution, and their attention.

Altar call: Make an altar call. Ask the children if any of them want to give their lives to Christ. Make the invitation.

Closing prayer: Model prayer. Ask one child to pray. Provide prompts. Pray for all the children, commit them into God's hands, and bless their week.

Review Lesson One to Six
Student Review and Practice Sheet

What is Routine? Routine is doing something over and over again till it becomes a part of you, till becomes a habit.

Our Routine

(1) Read your Bible   (4) Be helpful
(2) Pray   (5) Be thankful
(3) Be kind

Memory verse: Dan 6:10b (NLT): "He prayed three times a day, just as he had always done, giving thanks to his God."

Topic	What I learned
Introduction to Routine "But when Daniel learned that the law had been signed, he went home and knelt down as usual in his upstairs room, with its windows open toward Jerusalem. **He prayed three times a day, just as he had always done, giving thanks to his God**" (Daniel 6:10 NLT; bold added). *Do you have a routine? What is your routine?*	
Read Your Bible **"This Book of the Law shall not depart from your mouth, but you shall read [and meditate on] it day and night**, so that you may be careful to do [everything] in accordance with all that is written in it; for then you will make your way prosperous, and then you will be successful" (Joshua 1:8 AMP; bold added) *Do you read your Bible? What are the three things to ask God when you read your Bible?*	
Pray **"Pray continually** ..." (1 Thessalonians 5:17 NIV; bold added). *Which method do you use – The ACTS method or the Five Finger Prayer guide?*	

LESSON EIGHT

Be Kind, Be Helpful
The Good Samaritan
Teacher Guide

Introduction (10-15 minutes)

Welcome everyone to the class.

Check-in: Ask every child two questions.

1. How are you?
2. One fun question (You can select one from the list of fun questions on page x - xi).

Pray: Based on responses, pray for the specific needs of the children, and pray for the day's session.

Quick Review: Ask children about the previous lesson (which was a review). Find out if they remember, and if they completed their take home sheets.

Check for understanding of routine and ask whether they followed the suggested routine – Read your Bible, Pray, Be Kind, Be Helpful, and Be Thankful.

- **Reminder:** Routine is doing something over and over again till it becomes a part of you, till it becomes a habit.

Memory Verse: Daniel 6:10b (NLT): "He prayed three times a day, just as he had always done, giving thanks to his God."

Always Congratulate/Encourage them as needed.

The Main Lesson (30 -40 minutes)

Goals for the day

- Children will review the story of The Good Samaritan.
- Children will understand how to be helpful and kind from the parable of The Good Samaritan.

❖ Watch video (Optional) – Routine: Be helpful, Be kind (GeeDee Creative – YouTube).

Be Helpful, Be Kind.

Scriptures: The Good Samaritan – Luke 10:25-37, Ephesians 4:32a (AMP)

"Be kind and helpful to one another, tender-hearted [compassionate, understanding], forgiving one another [readily and freely], just as God in Christ also forgave you" (Luke 10:25-37, Ephesians 4:32a; bold added).

4. Discussion (guiding questions)

1. Who are the characters?
2. Who is a Samaritan? *The Samaritans were a group of people who lived in Samaria - an area north of Jerusalem. The Samaritans were half-Jews and half-Gentiles. When Assyria captured the northern kingdom of Israel in 721 B.C., some of them were taken in captivity, and others left behind. Those left behind intermarried with the Assyrians. This made them neither fully Hebrews nor fully Gentiles. At the time of Jesus, the Jews and the Samaritans did not deal with one another. They did not like one another.* [2]
3. Who is a Levite? (Levites were descendants of Levi, one of Jacob's sons. They performed different services in the temple of God. Some were priests, musicians, etc.).
4. Who is the most admirable person, and why?
5. Who was kind and helpful?
6. Why do you think the others did not help?
7. *Fun question – What would you have done?*

---

[2] (https://www.blueletterbible.org/faq/don_stewart/don_stewart_1319.cfm)

Reinforcing Activities (included resources and materials needed)

Select any or all the listed activities for the children to work on.

- Bible
- Pencils and pens
- Construction sheet/plain sheet/notebook
- Coloring sheet – Be Helpful, Be Kind
- Coloring sheet (2) – The Good Samaritan
- Coloring verse– Luke 10:36-37
- Word search (2) – Ages 6-10, 10-14
- Student review and practice sheet

Conclusion (10 – 15 minutes)

Check for understanding: Ask each child what they learned and how they are going to apply it in their lives.

Life-Giver challenge: Each child will list five ways s/he will be helpful and kind this week. *Remind the children to continue tracking their routine.*

Affirmation: Let the children know how proud you are of them and appreciate their participation, their contribution, and their attention.

Altar call: Make an altar call. Ask the children if any of them want to give their lives to Christ. Make the invitation.

Closing prayer: Model prayer. Ask one child to pray. Provide prompts. Pray for all the children, commit them into God's hands, and bless their week.

Be Kind, Be Helpful
The Good Samaritan
Student Review and Practice Sheet

What is Routine? Routine is doing something over and over again till it becomes a part of you, till it becomes a habit.

Our Routine

(1) Read your bible
(2) Pray
(3) Be kind
(4) Be helpful
(5) Be thankful

Read: Luke 10:25-37–The Good Samaritan

Memory verse: Dan 6: 10b (NLT): "He prayed three times a day, just as he had always done, giving thanks to his God."

Life-Giver challenge: List 5 ways you will be helpful and kind this week.

What I learned today:

_____

_____

_____

What I plan to do:

_____

_____

_____

LESSON EIGHT

Be Helpful, Be Kind

The Good Samaritan. Version 1

The Good Samaritan. Version 2

Be Helpful, Be Kind
The Good Samaritan
(ages 6 –10)

Word List

1. Other   2. Pray   3. Care   4. Wine   5. Help   6. Bible   7. Read   8. Kind
9. Thieves   10. Levite   11. Share   12. Oil   13. Good   14. Each   15. Priest

C	D	B	X	C	G	J	C	C	H	X	X	Q	Z	L	P
R	W	S	C	B	S	H	A	R	E	J	I	O	S	O	X
E	Q	R	Z	G	T	L	R	U	L	Z	X	H	T	O	W
C	J	F	X	O	T	H	E	R	P	D	E	Z	E	X	A
V	D	Q	V	O	H	Z	A	V	U	N	Z	T	N	L	N
Z	Y	Q	R	D	I	D	D	C	I	Q	C	E	T	V	C
A	P	S	V	L	E	F	O	W	N	T	Q	S	X	I	M
A	E	U	U	F	V	X	N	F	D	B	E	J	C	L	P
F	Z	V	B	G	E	X	R	I	N	I	A	U	J	H	Z
N	N	Z	X	W	S	C	P	D	R	B	C	R	Z	J	I
L	E	Q	P	Z	R	N	H	P	E	L	H	G	G	F	S
L	K	Z	Q	E	D	N	J	R	A	E	K	M	G	K	Z
G	F	O	N	N	A	V	L	A	D	O	A	M	T	V	T
B	S	O	I	D	W	A	S	Y	G	I	G	L	M	C	Y
Z	D	K	P	L	Z	V	F	T	Q	J	U	E	M	L	U
S	E	G	S	O	F	P	L	Z	F	N	M	N	D	R	A

Be Helpful, Be Kind
The Good Samaritan
(ages 10–14)

Word List

1. Good   2. Care   3. Innkeeper   4. Steal   5. Priest   6. Neighbor   7. Samaritan
8. Pray   9. Read   10. Bible   11. Attack   12. Thieves   13. Ephesians   14. Wine
15. Luke   16. Wounds   17. Share   18. Oil   19. Levite   20. Routine

```
Y  V  Y  R  N  V  B  Y  X  K  D  P  Z  K  P  A
C  S  M  E  P  H  E  S  I  A  N  S  A  K  U  I
H  J  U  P  K  Y  W  P  R  I  E  S  T  C  J  T
Y  F  F  X  E  W  N  X  M  Y  K  Q  T  E  X  L
F  I  N  N  K  E  E  P  E  R  P  R  A  Y  A  Z
L  I  G  Q  T  R  I  L  S  H  T  P  C  N  O  L
W  Y  K  D  A  C  G  U  A  B  K  Q  K  U  F  S
W  F  V  C  Z  L  H  J  M  R  J  X  O  P  Z  P
Q  M  Q  H  Q  R  B  L  A  P  J  L  P  Z  Y  G
B  V  H  V  W  E  O  B  R  W  O  U  N  D  S  O
O  F  G  Q  L  A  R  U  I  K  L  K  K  X  L  O
W  J  X  B  D  D  Q  H  T  H  I  E  V  E  S  D
I  L  I  N  M  I  L  C  A  I  N  Z  V  O  I  P
I  B  G  G  W  Y  P  C  N  I  N  V  N  I  W  A
K  S  Y  F  B  S  W  U  W  B  S  E  F  L  T  Y
R  Q  P  I  V  N  L  Y  O  W  Q  S  H  A  R  E
```

LESSON NINE

Be Kind, Be Helpful
A 21st Century Good Samaritan
Teacher Guide

Introduction (10 Minutes)

Welcome everyone to the class.

Check-in: Ask every child two questions.

1. How are you?
2. One fun question (You can select one from the list of fun questions on page x - xi).

Pray: Based on responses, pray for the specific needs of the children, and pray for the day's session.

Check for understanding of routine and ask whether they followed the suggested routine – Read your Bible, Pray, Be Kind, Be Helpful, and Be Thankful.

- **Reminder:** Routine is doing something over and over again till it becomes a part of you, till it becomes a habit.

Quick Review: Previous lesson and challenge on 'Be kind, Be helpful. The parable of the Good Samaritan.

Memory verse: Dan 6: 10b (NLT): "He prayed three times a day, just as he had always done, giving thanks to his God."

Congratulate/Encourage as needed.

The Main Lesson (30 - 40 minutes)

Goals for the day

- Children will review the story of the Good Samaritan (Luke 10:25-37).
- Children will review a 21ˢᵗ Century story of a Good Samaritan.
- Children will consider the importance of being a Good Samaritan.

❖ Watch video (Optional) – Routine: Be helpful, Be kind (GeeDee Creative – YouTube).

Be Helpful, Be Kind (Part 2). A 21ˢᵗ Century Good Samaritan

Scriptures: "Be kind and helpful to one another, tender-hearted [compassionate, understanding], forgiving one another [readily and freely], just as God in Christ also forgave you" (Ephesians 4:32a AMP; bold added).

A 21ˢᵗ Century Good Samaritan - This story of kindness was carried on many news media and social media on April 8, 2020. During the 2020 Pandemic (Corona Virus Outbreak), a very rich man paid for the most vulnerable people at 73 Winn-Dixie and Kroger shops in the USA. Winn-Dixie's had a special hour for elderly and high-risk shoppers at all 29 Winn-Dixie locations in Louisiana and 44 Kroger grocery stores around the Atlanta area. On that morning, as the shoppers got to the cashier to pay for their grocery, they were all pleasantly surprised to learn that someone had paid for them. He had paid for all their groceries!!! There were many reactions. How would you have reacted?

Discussion (guiding questions)

1. Who are the characters?
2. How is this 21ˢᵗ century Good Samaritan like the parable of the Good Samaritan?
3. Why is this story important?
4. What did it mean for those who received the kindness/help?
5. Can you imagine and describe how they felt?
6. Fun question – Have you been a Good Samaritan in the past week or month? What did you do?

Reinforcing Activities (included resources and materials needed)

Select any or all the listed activities for the children to work on.

- Bible
- Pencils and pens
- Construction sheet/plain sheet/notebook
- Coloring sheet – The 21st Century Good Samaritan
- Coloring verse – Ephesians 4:32a
- Match the verse activity
- Student review and practice sheet

Conclusion (10 – 15 minutes)

Check for understanding – Ask each child what they learned and how they are going to apply it in their lives.

Life-Giver challenge – Each child will research or look for other 21st century Good Samaritans. *Remind the children to continue tracking their routines.*

Affirmation - Let the children know how proud you are of them – appreciate their participation, their contribution, and their attention.

Altar call: Make an altar call. Ask the children if any of them want to give their lives to Christ. Make the invitation.

Closing prayer: Model prayer. Ask one child to pray. Provide prompts. Pray for all the children, commit them into God's hands, and bless their week.

Be Kind, Be Helpful
A 21st Century Good Samaritan
Student Review and Practice Sheet

What is Routine? Routine is doing something over and over again till it becomes a part of you, till it becomes a habit.

Our Routine

(1) Read your Bible
(2) Pray
(3) Be kind
(4) Be helpful
(5) Be thankful

Read: Ephesians 4:32a

Memory verse: Dan 6:10b (NLT): "He prayed three times a day, just as he had always done, giving thanks to his God."

Life-Giver challenge: Look for a current day (21st century) Good Samaritan.

What I learned today:

_____

_____

_____

What I plan to do:

_____

_____

_____

Ephesians 4:32a AMP

A 21st Century Good Samaritan

Be Kind. Be Helpful
Match the Verse Activity
[Look up the verse and match it].

BIBLE VERSES – Galatians 5:22-23(NLT). Proverbs 19:17(NIV). Galatians 6:10 (NIV). Acts 20:35 (NKJV). 1 Corinthians 13:4 (NIV). Ephesians 4:32 (AMP). Romans 12:13 (NLT). Hebrews 6:10 (NIV). Proverbs 3:27 (NLT). Hebrews 13:16 (NKJV).

1. "Love is patient, love is kind. It does not envy, it does not boast, it is not proud."
2. "Be kind *and* helpful to one another, tender-hearted [compassionate, understanding], forgiving one another [readily and freely], just as God in Christ also forgave you."
3. "Therefore, as we have opportunity, let us do good to all people, especially to those who belong to the family of believers."
4. "But the Holy Spirit produces this kind of fruit in our lives: love, joy, peace, patience, kindness, goodness, faithfulness, gentleness, and self-control. There is no law against these things!"
5. "I have shown you in every way, by laboring like this, that you must support the weak. And remember the words of the Lord Jesus, that He said, 'It is more blessed to give than to receive."
6. "And don't forget to do good and to share with those in need. These are the sacrifices that please God."
7. "Whoever is kind to the poor lends to the Lord, and he will reward them for what they have done."
8. "When God's people are in need, be ready to help them. Always be eager to practice hospitality."
9. "God is not unjust; he will not forget your work and the love you have shown him as you have helped his people and continue to help them."
10. "Do not withhold good from those who deserve it when it's in your power to help them."

Be Thankful –Ten Healed of Leprosy Teacher Guide

Introduction (10 – 15 minutes)

Welcome everyone to the class.

Check-in: Ask every child two questions.

1. How are you?
2. One fun question (You can select one from the list of fun questions on page x - xi).

Pray: Based on responses, pray for the specific needs of the children, and pray for the day's session.

Check for understanding of routine and ask whether they followed the suggested routine – Read your Bible, Pray, Be Kind, Be Helpful, and Be Thankful.

- **Reminder:** Routine is doing something over and over again till it becomes a part of you, till it becomes a habit.

Quick Review: Previous lesson and challenge – "Be kind, Be helpful. A 21st Century Good Samaritan."

Memory verse: Daniel 6:10b (NLT): "He prayed three times a day, just as he had always done, giving thanks to his God."

Always Congratulate/Encourage them as needed.

The Main Lesson (30 minutes)

Goals for the day

- Children will be familiar with the Ten Lepers who were healed in Luke's account.
- Children will discuss the importance of being thankful.
- Children will share ways they will be thankful.

❖ Watch video (Optional) – Routine: Be Thankful (GeeDee Creative – YouTube).

Be Thankful

Probing Questions

- What does it mean to be thankful?
- Why is it important to be thankful?
- What are the ways to show that you are thankful?

Scriptures: Ten healed of leprosy Luke 17:11-19 (NLT), Colossians 3:15 (NLT)

Discussion (guiding questions)

1. What is leprosy? Who is a leper?
2. Why were the lepers crying out to Jesus?
3. Why do you think Jesus told them to show themselves to the priests?
4. What happened on the way to show themselves to the priests?
5. Why do you think only one returned to say thank you?
6. Why was Jesus pleased with the one who came back to say thank you? *He was a Samaritan. Who is a Samaritan? Tip – The Parable of the Good Samaritan. Remember – The Samaritans and Jews hated each other.*
7. Fun question – Why do you think the others didn't come back?

Reinforcing Activities (included resources and materials needed)

Select any or all the listed activities for the children to work on.

- Bible
- Pencils and pens
- Construction Sheet/plain sheet/notebooks
- Coloring sheet (2) –The Ten Lepers (Older and Younger children)

- Coloring verse – Colossians 3:15
- Word search (2) – Ages 6-10, 10-15
- Student review and practice sheet

Conclusion (10 – 15 minutes)

Check for understanding – Ask each child what they learned and how they are going to apply it in their lives.

Life-Giver challenge – Each child will list five people who helped them during this or the past school year. He/she will write thank you note or make a thank you card for them. *Remind the children to continue tracking their routines.*

Affirmation - Let the children know how proud you are of them and appreciate their participation, their contribution, and their attention.

Altar call: Make an altar call. Ask the children if any of them want to give their lives to Christ. Make the invitation.

Closing prayer: Model prayer. Ask one child to pray. Provide prompts. Pray for all the children, commit them into God's hands, and bless their week.

Be Thankful –Ten Healed of Leprosy Student review and practice sheet

What is Routine? Routine is doing something over and over again till it becomes a part of you, till it becomes a habit.

Our Routine

    (1) Read your Bible
    (2) Pray
    (3) Be kind
    (4) Be helpful
    (5) Be thankful

Read: Luke 17:11-19 (NLT) –Ten Healed of Leprosy, Colossians 3:15

Memorize: Dan 6:10b (NLT): "He prayed three times a day, just as he had always done, giving thanks to his God."

Life-Giver challenge: List five people who have helped you during this school year. Write a thank you note or make a thank you card for them.

What I learned today:

_____

_____

_____

What I plan to do:

_____

_____

_____

Colossians 3:15 NLT

Ten Healed. Only One returns to say Thank You. Version 1

Ten Healed. Only One returns to say Thank You. Version 2

Be Thankful –Ten Healed of Leprosy (ages 6–10)

Word List

1. Stand 2. Love 3. Kind 4. Pray 5. Jesus 6. Faith 7. Habit 8. Heal
9. Mercy 10. One 11. Glory 12. Lepers 13. Ten 14. Nine 15. Only

H	R	E	E	O	B	U	Q	U	H	N	K	Q	G	A	X
Q	D	G	U	L	D	Q	K	T	E	N	N	U	W	B	Y
G	Q	V	K	H	L	C	I	R	H	A	B	I	T	J	M
Z	Q	C	F	P	S	A	N	I	N	E	L	S	R	M	A
X	Q	Y	Q	C	F	R	D	N	R	R	A	T	E	S	S
O	W	P	F	Y	P	V	Z	T	U	U	U	L	U	A	L
O	V	B	C	F	O	Y	J	E	E	Z	W	U	F	U	O
A	S	T	U	X	K	R	S	N	C	F	T	B	R	B	D
W	D	V	B	G	Z	L	O	V	E	W	P	Q	Z	D	T
F	X	T	L	T	J	E	S	U	S	V	G	Z	B	B	A
X	Q	T	V	T	Y	P	V	T	I	D	X	X	F	D	S
Z	E	O	P	R	P	E	D	D	A	C	V	T	Q	M	V
I	U	A	O	G	L	R	B	B	V	N	D	Y	K	M	D
D	T	L	I	N	V	S	A	G	W	Z	D	T	B	M	O
G	G	Q	V	Y	L	Z	E	Y	D	A	H	Z	K	B	I
X	M	M	E	R	C	Y	V	D	I	P	A	T	B	L	A

Be Thankful –Ten Healed of Leprosy (ages 10–14)

Word List

1. Lepers 2. Samaria 3. Read 4. Nine 5. Heal 6. Habit 7. Routine
8. Thankful 9. Kind 10. Faith 11. Jesus 12. Priests 13. Always 14. Show
15. Pray 16. Glory 17. Master 18. Praise 19. Stand 20. Mercy

```
P  N  J  N  I  P  A  L  D  Z  E  X  B  U  G  B
M  R  E  A  B  X  B  F  Z  S  S  F  R  D  G  U
U  Y  I  L  J  P  O  L  D  Y  E  H  Z  V  I  H
L  I  R  E  E  C  P  N  A  N  G  P  E  O  M  S
G  K  E  O  S  H  A  B  I  T  I  K  U  P  J  I
I  W  A  F  U  T  J  N  M  Z  P  E  R  L  Q  O
X  B  D  G  S  T  S  P  A  T  T  Q  A  E  Q  D
E  K  N  C  F  H  I  F  S  E  F  E  G  P  F  B
E  R  P  M  A  F  T  N  T  L  H  G  L  E  Z  D
Z  W  O  Z  K  A  H  Q  E  R  L  P  O  R  M  Q
S  A  M  A  R  I  A  S  R  Q  O  P  R  S  T  E
M  F  Y  U  T  T  N  Z  H  B  T  R  Y  A  L  Y
M  O  K  F  L  H  K  D  U  O  O  A  I  N  Y  R
M  D  I  V  N  M  F  O  W  T  W  I  N  P  R  H
Z  F  K  O  F  R  U  G  X  L  J  S  O  X  C  K
F  L  Z  R  C  H  L  B  A  B  M  E  R  C  Y  R
```

LESSON ELEVEN

Be Thankful–Hannah's Prayer of Praise Teacher Guide

Introduction (10 – 15 minutes)

Welcome everyone to the class.

Check-in: Ask every child two questions.

1. How are you?
2. (You can select one from the list of fun questions on page x - xi).

Pray: Based on responses, pray for the specific needs of the children, and pray for the day's session.

Check for understanding of routine and ask whether they followed the suggested routine – Read your Bible, Pray, Be Kind, Be Helpful, and Be Thankful.

- **Reminder:** Routine is doing something over and over again till it becomes a part of you, till it becomes a habit.

Quick Review: Previous lesson and challenge on 'Be Thankful. A 21ˢᵗ Century Good Samaritan.'

Memory verse: Daniel 6:10b (NLT): "He prayed three times a day, just as he had always done, giving thanks to his God."

Always Congratulate/Encourage them as needed.

The Main Lesson (30 -40 minutes)

Goals for the day

- Children will be familiar with Hannah's prayer of praise in 1Sam 2:1-10.
- Children will discuss the importance of being thankful.
- Children will share ways that they are thankful for God's goodness to them.

❖ Watch video (Optional) – Routine: Be Thankful (GeeDee Creative – YouTube).

Be Thankful

Probing Questions

- What does it mean to be thankful?
- What are some other words for thankful?
- Why is it important to be thankful?
- What happens when you are not thankful?

Scriptures: 1 Sam 1:1-11, 1 Sam 2:1-10, Psalm 105:1

1 Sam 2:1-2 (`NLT) - Then Hannah prayed: "My heart rejoices in the Lord! The Lord has made me strong. Now I have an answer for my enemies; I rejoice because you rescued me. 2 No one is holy like the Lord! There is no one besides you; there is no Rock like our God."

Discussion (guiding questions)

1. How many wives did Elkanah have?
2. Can you describe Hannah and Peninnah?
3. Why was Hannah sad?
4. What did Hannah ask God for? (Remind the children that Hannah was specific)
5. How did God answer Hannah's prayer?
6. What do you think about Hannah's thanksgiving prayer?
7. Do you remember the Leper who came by to say thank you?

Reinforcing Activities (included resources and materials needed)

Select any or all the listed activities for the children to work on.

- Bible
- Pencils and pens
- Construction sheet/plain sheet/notebook
- Coloring sheet – Hannah's Prayer of Praise
- Coloring verse– Psalm 105:1
- Match the verse activity
- Student review and practice sheet

Conclusion (10 – 15 minutes)

Check for understanding – Ask each child what they learned and how they are going to apply it in their lives.

Life-Giver challenge – Ask children to write a poem or a letter, like Hannah, to express their gratitude. *Remind the children to continue tracking their routines.*

- ***Show and Tell for the next time you meet*** – Ask children to bring their best take home activity sheet. Inform children that they will present their best/favorite challenge to the class.

Affirmation - Let the children know how proud you are of them and appreciate their participation, their contribution, and their attention.

Altar call: Make an altar call. Ask the children if any of them want to give their lives to Christ. Make the invitation.

Closing prayer: Model prayer. Ask one child to pray. Provide prompts. Pray for all the children, commit them into God's hands, and bless their week.

Be Thankful – Hannah's Prayer of Praise
Student Review and Practice

What is Routine? Routine is doing something over and over again till it becomes a part of you, till it becomes a habit.

Our Routine

(1) Read your Bible
(2) Pray
(3) Be kind
(4) Be helpful
(5) Be thankful

Read: 1 Samuel 2:1-10 (Hannah's prayer of praise)

Memorize: Dan 6:10b (NLT): "He prayed three times a day, just as he had always done, giving thanks to his God."

Life-Giver challenge: Using Hannah's song as an example, write a poem or a letter to express your thankfulness/gratitude to God.

Show and Tell for the next time you meet. Bring your best take home activity sheet. You will present it to the class.

What I learned today:

_____
_____
_____

What I plan to do:

_____
_____
_____

Psalm 105:1 NLT

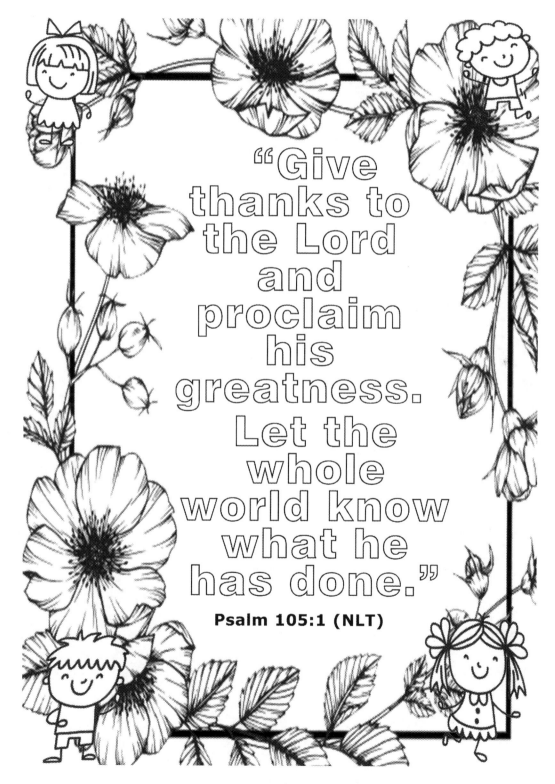

"Give thanks to the Lord and proclaim his greatness. Let the whole world know what he has done."

Psalm 105:1 (NLT)

Hannah's Prayer of Praise

Be Thankful
Match the Verse Activity
[Look up the verse and match it].

BIBLE VERSES - 1 Chronicles 16:8 (NKJV). Colossians 3:15 (NIV). Psalm 106:1 (NKJV). Thessalonians 5:18 (NLT). Ephesians 5:20 (AMP). Philippians 4:6-7 (NLT). Hebrews 13:15 (AMP). Hebrews 12:28-29 (NLT Colossians 4:2 (NIV). Psalm 100:4(AMP).

1. "Be thankful in all circumstances, for this is God's will for you who belong to Christ Jesus."
2. "Let the peace of Christ rule in your hearts, since as members of one body you were called to peace. And be thankful."
3. "Devote yourselves to prayer, being watchful and thankful."
4. "Don't worry about anything; instead, pray about everything. Tell God what you need and thank him for all he has done. Then you will experience God's peace, which exceeds anything we can understand. His peace will guard your hearts and minds as you live in Christ Jesus."
5. "Praise the Lord! Oh, give thanks to the Lord, for *He is* good! For His mercy *endures* forever."
6. "Through Him, therefore, let us at all times offer up to God a sacrifice of praise, which is the fruit of lips that thankfully acknowledge *and* confess *and* glorify His name."
7. "Oh, give thanks to the Lord! Call upon His name; Make known His deeds among the peoples!"
8. "Enter His gates with a song of thanksgiving and His courts with praise. Be thankful to Him, bless *and* praise His name."
9. "Since we are receiving a Kingdom that is unshakable, let us be thankful and please God by worshiping him with holy fear and awe. For our God is a devouring fire."
10. "…always giving thanks to God the Father for all things, in the name of our Lord Jesus Christ."

Which is your favorite verse? Why do you like this verse?

LESSON TWELVE

Routine Grand Finale-
Review and Awards
Teacher Guide

Introduction (5 – 10 minutes)

Welcome everyone to the class.

- Check-in: Ask every child two questions.

  1. How are you?
  2. One fun question (You can select one from the list of fun questions on page x - xi).

- Pray: Based on responses, pray for the specific needs of the children, and pray for the day's session.

Check for understanding of routine and ask whether they followed the suggested routine – Read your Bible, Pray, Be Kind, Be Helpful, and Be Thankful.

- **Reminder:** Routine is doing something over and over again till it becomes a part of you, till it becomes a habit.

Memory verse: Daniel 6:10b (NLT): "He prayed three times a day, just as he had always done, giving thanks to his God."

The Main Lesson (40 minutes)

Goals for the day

- Children will discuss and share their learnings on Routine.
- Children will share what they learned during the past eleven weeks.
- Children will share some of their best work.
- Children will receive their certificates.

❖ Watch video (Optional) – Routine: Be Thankful (GeeDee Creative – YouTube). (*This video is useful for a review of all the lessons*).

Review Lessons One through Eleven

Probing Questions

- What does Routine mean to you?
- Do you have a Routine?
- What have you done with –

  o Read your Bible
  o Pray
  o Be Helpful
  o Be Kind
  o Be Thankful

- What was your best Life-Giver challenge?

Scriptures: Daniel 6:10 (NLT), Joshua 1:8 (AMP, 1 Thessalonians 5:17 (NIV), Ephesians 4:32a (AMP), Colossians 3:15 (NLT)

- "But when Daniel learned that the law had been signed, he went home and knelt down as usual in his room upstairs, with its windows open toward Jerusalem. **He prayed three times a day, just as he had always done, giving thanks to his God**" (Daniel 6:10 NLT; bold added)
- "**This Book of the Law shall not depart from your mouth, but you shall read [and meditate on] it day and night**, so that you may be careful to do [everything] in accordance with all that is written in it; for then you will make your way prosperous, and then you will be successful" (Joshua 1:8 AMP; bold added)

- "**Pray continually,**" (1 Thessalonians 5:17 NIV; bold added)
- "**Be kind and helpful to one another, tender-hearted ...**" (Ephesians 4:32a AMP; bold added)
- "**And always be thankful ...**" (Colossians 3:15 NLT; bold added)

❖ **Show and Tell Activity** – Each child will share their best/favorite "Life-Giver challenge" from the weeks. Children will explain why it is their favorite and what they plan to do.

The Supplies Needed

- Bible
- Notebook
- Pencils and pens
- Student review and practice sheet
- Certificate of attendance and participation (for the children)

Conclusion (10-15 minutes)

Awards and Recognition – Affirmation: Let the children know how proud you are of them – appreciate their participation, their contribution, and their attention. **Each child will receive a certificate of attendance and appreciation.**

Altar Call: Make an altar call. Ask the children if any of them want to give their lives to Christ. Make the invitation.

Closing Prayer: Model prayer. Ask one child to pray. Provide prompts. Pray for all the children, commit them into God's hands, and bless their week.

LESSON TWELVE

Grand Finale
Student Review and Practice

What is Routine? Routine is doing something over and over again till it becomes a part of you, till it becomes a habit.

Our Routine

(1) Read your Bible　　(4) Be helpful
(2) Pray　　(5) Be thankful
(3) Be kind

Memory verse: Dan 6:10b (NLT): "He prayed three times a day, just as he had always done, giving thanks to his God."

Topic	What I learned ...
Introduction to Routine **"He prayed three times a day, just as he had always done, giving thanks to his God"** (Daniel 6:10 NLT; bold added) *Write out your daily routine.*	
Read Your Bible **"This Book of the Law shall not depart from your mouth, but you shall read [and meditate on] it day and night, ..."** (Joshua 1:8 AMP; bold added) *Keep a journal of your Bible reading.*	
Pray **"Pray continually ..."** (1 Thessalonians 5:17 NIV; bold added) *Using the Five Finger Prayer, make a list of people you will be praying for.*	
Be Helpful, and Be Kind **"Be kind and helpful to one another, tender-hearted ..."** (Ephesians 4:32a AMP; bold added) *Find ways to be helpful and kind.*	
Be Thankful **"And always be thankful"** (Colossians 3:15 NLT; bold added) *At the end of each day, write down one thing you are thankful for.*	

Read your Bible, Pray, Be Helpful, Be Kind, Be Thankful

CERTIFICATE

OF PARTICIPATION

This award is presented to

_____

for Participation in

A ROUTINE FOR LIFE CURRICULUM

(DANIEL 6:10)

PRESENTED BY:

ON THIS DAY:

Read your Bible, Pray, Be Helpful, Be Kind, Be Thankful

ANSWER KEY FOR WORD PUZZLES

LESSON ONE – (AGES 6 – 10)

LESSON ONE - (AGES 10–14)

LESSON TWO – (AGES 6 – 10)

LESSON TWO – (AGES 10 – 14)

LESSON THREE – (AGES 6–10)

LESSON THREE – (AGES 10–14)

LESSON FOUR - (AGES 6–10)

LESSON FOUR - (AGES 10–14)

ANSWER KEY FOR WORD PUZZLES

LESSON FIVE – (AGES 6–10)

LESSON FIVE – (AGES 10–14)

LESSON SIX – (AGES 6–10)

LESSON SIX – (AGES 10–14)

LESSON EIGHT – (AGES 6 –10)

LESSON EIGHT – (AGES 10 –14)

LESSON TEN – (AGES 6–10)

LESSON TEN – (AGES 10–14)

Be Kind, Be Helpful
Match the Verse Activity

1. "Love is patient, love is kind. It does not envy, it does not boast, it is not proud." **1 Corinthians 13:4 (NIV)**

2. "Be kind *and* helpful to one another, tender-hearted [compassionate, understanding], forgiving one another [readily and freely], just as God in Christ also forgave you." **Ephesians 4:32 (AMP).**

3. "Therefore, as we have opportunity, let us do good to all people, especially to those who belong to the family of believers." **Galatians 6:10 (NIV).**

4. "But the Holy Spirit produces this kind of fruit in our lives: love, joy, peace, patience, kindness, goodness, faithfulness, gentleness, and self-control. There is no law against these things!" **Galatians 5:22-23 (NLT).**

5. "I have shown you in every way, by laboring like this, that you must support the weak. And remember the words of the Lord Jesus, that He said, 'It is more blessed to give than to receive." **Acts 20:35 (NKJV).**

6. "And don't forget to do good and to share with those in need. These are the sacrifices that please God." **Hebrews 13:16 (NKJV).**

7. "Whoever is kind to the poor lends to the Lord, and he will reward them for what they have done." **Proverbs 19:17 (NIV).**

8. "When God's people are in need, be ready to help them. Always be eager to practice hospitality." **Romans 12:13 (NLT).**

9. "God is not unjust; he will not forget your work and the love you have shown him as you have helped his people and continue to help them." **Hebrews 6:10 (NIV).**

10. "Do not withhold good from those who deserve it when it's in your power to help them." **Proverbs 3:27 (NLT).**

1=1 Corinthians 13:4 (NIV). 2= Ephesians 4:32 (AMP). 3= Galatians 6:10 (NIV). 4= Galatians 5:22-23(NLT). 5= Acts 20:35 (NKJV). 6= Hebrews 13:16 (NKJV). 7= Proverbs 19:17(NIV). 8= Romans 12:13 (NLT). 9= Hebrews 6:10 (NIV). 10= Proverbs 3:27 (NLT).

Be Thankful
Match the Verse Activity

1. "Be thankful in all circumstances, for this is God's will for you who belong to Christ Jesus." 1 **Thessalonians 5:18 (NLT)**.

2. "Let the peace of Christ rule in your hearts, since as members of one body you were called to peace. And be thankful." **Colossians 3:15 (NIV)**.

3. "Devote yourselves to prayer, being watchful and thankful." **Colossians 4:2 (NIV)**.

4. "Don't worry about anything; instead, pray about everything. Tell God what you need and thank him for all he has done. Then you will experience God's peace, which exceeds anything we can understand. His peace will guard your hearts and minds as you live in Christ Jesus." **Philippians 4:6-7 (NLT)**.

5. "Praise the Lord! Oh, give thanks to the Lord, for *He is* good! For His mercy *endures* forever." **Psalm 106:1 (NKJV)**.

6. "Through Him, therefore, let us at all times offer up to God a sacrifice of praise, which is the fruit of lips that thankfully acknowledge *and* confess *and* glorify His name." **Hebrews 13:15 (AMP)**.

7. "Oh, give thanks to the Lord! Call upon His name; Make known His deeds among the peoples!" 1 **Chronicles 16:8 (NKJV)**.

8. "Enter His gates with a song of thanksgiving and His courts with praise. Be thankful to Him, bless *and* praise His name." **Psalm 100:4(AMP)**.

9. "Since we are receiving a Kingdom that is unshakable, let us be thankful and please God by worshiping him with holy fear and awe. For our God is a devouring fire." **Hebrews 12:28-29 (NLT)**.

10. "… always giving thanks to God the Father for all things, in the name of our Lord Jesus Christ." **Ephesians 5:20 (AMP)**.

1= **Thessalonians 5:18 (NLT)**. 2= **Colossians 3:15 (NIV)**. 3= **Colossians 4:2 (NIV)**. 4= **Philippians 4:6-7 (NLT)**. 5= **Psalm 106:1 (NKJV)**. 6= **Hebrews 13:15 (AMP)**. 7= **Chronicles 16:8 (NKJV)**. 8= **Psalm 100:4(AMP)**. 9= **Hebrews 12:28-29 (NLT)**. 10= **Ephesians 5:20 (AMP)**.

Printed in the United States
by Baker & Taylor Publisher Services